THE SALEM WITCH

MW01010061

Katherine W. Richardson

PEABODY ESSEX MUSEUM

SALEM, MASSACHUSETTS   1994

Library of Congress Catalogue Card Number
83-81118

International Standard Book Number
0-88389-089-5

First Edition 1983
Second Printing 1984
Third Printing 1986
Fourth Printing 1988
Fifth Printing 1990
Sixth Printing 1992
Seventh Printing 1994

Designed by Sandra Rigney

Produced by The Book Department, Inc.,
Boston, Massachusetts

Composition by Foster-Bush Studio,
Wellesley, Massachusetts

Printed at Daamen Printing,
West Rutland, Vermont

Publication expenses have been met by the James Duncan Phillips Fund.

Printed in the United States of America

ACKNOWLEDGMENTS

A number of people helped in the preparation of this book by checking the text, clarifying historical points, and suggesting sources of information: Anne Farnam, curator, Essex Institute; K. David Goss, coordinator of education, Essex Institute; Stephen W. Herring, curator of the Framingham Historical and Natural History Society, Framingham, Massachusetts; Mrs. Arthur R. Norton, reference librarian, Essex Institute; Caroline Preston, manuscript librarian, Essex Institute; Marshall W. S. Swan, president, Essex County Historical Association; and Richard B. Trask, town archivist, Town of Danvers, Massachusetts, Archival Center.

Katherine W. Richardson
Managing Editor,
Essex Institute Historical Collections
August 1983

CONTENTS

INTRODUCTION

The Salem witchcraft hysteria of 1692 was a bleak episode in Massachusetts history. Triggered by a series of childish experiments in sorcery and magic, the situation swiftly grew into an epidemic of fear and horror that culminated in bitter courtroom trials, the death of twenty-four individuals (nineteen of them by hanging), and the imprisonment of over 200.

Today, nearly three centuries after the Salem spectacle, the trials seem ancient history, but they still evoke endless interest and curiosity. Salem has long attracted historians and visitors who want to examine the phenomenon close to the original site. A few artifacts from the witchcraft proceedings are still in existence today, and some of the buildings associated with those who played a role in the trials remain. The most significant material from the witchcraft trials, however, is the large collection of original manuscripts documenting the court testimony. The papers, now housed in the manuscript library of the Peabody Essex Museum, have been a source of study for many generations of scholars.*

Superstitious beliefs in evil gods and magic spells date back to pre-Christian times, but the great struggle of the church (both Catholic and Protestant) and of the state to defeat Satan and his demonic powers reached epic proportions in Europe during the fifteenth, sixteenth, and seventeenth centuries.

A witch was considered to be one who had agreed to serve the Devil by performing evil acts in the world. Supposedly, witches would make a contract with Satan by signing in his book, and would thereafter have amazing powers to fly through the air, perform great feats of strength, change appearance, and cause mis-

---

*In 1977 the complete courtroom records were published (Paul Boyer and Stephen Nissenbaum, *The Salem Witchcraft Papers*, 3 vols. [New York: Da Capo Press, 1977]). The volumes may be found in many public libraries.

fortune or death to their victims. Witches worked alone or with "familiar" animal companions, and it was said that they often congregated by night in groups or covens to hold a witches' sabbath, a depraved festival of devil-worshipping ceremonies, feasting, and sorcery. Witchcraft was an evil form of religion practiced by heretics; it was therefore a threat to Christianity, and every Christian nation devised laws to control it. In Toulouse, France, forty witches were burned to death in 1557. In Germany the persecution of supposed witches was particularly intense—many thousands lost their lives between 1550 and 1650, and 133 were burned in one day in the year 1589. In England, 19 persons were convicted and hanged as witches in 1645. Thus the subject of witchcraft was a universal topic in the 1600s, and Puritan New England and Salem shared these deeply felt moral and religious concerns.

According to the earliest colonial laws, witchcraft in America was punishable by death; the total number of "witches" executed in America was only thirty-six, but twenty of that unfortunate number were put to death in Salem in the span of a single year.

There had been a number of isolated witchcraft cases tried in New England before 1692, some of them as early as 1658, 1662, and 1665. In 1688 the children of John Goodwin of Boston became hysterically ill and accused a woman named Glover, an Irish immigrant who was the mother of their family servant, of witchcraft. Glover was tried and hanged. Cotton Mather, a highly respected minister at the Second, or North Church, in Boston, interviewed and studied the Goodwin children extensively in the belief that the details of this case would increase his general understanding of the mysterious nature of witchcraft. Mather published his findings in *Memorable Providences, Relating to Witchcrafts and Possessions,* a widely circulated book that described in full the sorcery and magic experiments conducted by Mary Glover.

SALEM VILLAGE IN 1691

In Salem Village (now part of Danvers, Massachusetts) participation in "black magic" experiments was confined at first to a group of several young girls who engaged in superstitious games as a frivolous pastime. Little Betty Parris, the nine-year-old daughter of the new Village minister, Samuel Parris, and her cousin, Abigail Williams, aged eleven, spent much time in the company of the Parris family's West Indian slave, Tituba, who may well have amused the children with her fortune-telling and her Barbados tales of voodoo spells and witches.

Salem Village was a parish of Salem Town, but still considered under the legal jurisdiction of the larger Town. There was, consequently, some friction between the two communities as the Village sought to become independent of the Town. Even within the Village itself, there was considerable dissension between neighbors over boundary lines, property, and other matters, including the choice of a preacher for their meeting house (there were four different ministers between 1672 and 1697). The Reverend Samuel Parris, Betty's father, became the Village minister in 1688 and was a subject of controversy among the various Village factions. Feelings concerning his ministry were particularly strong in 1690 and 1691, just prior to the outbreak of the witchcraft episode.

As winter approached and the days grew colder, Parris's shed became the gathering place for a group of bored and restless young girls. These Salem Village children had little to occupy their time but the drudgery of routine indoor tasks and the strict demands of their Calvinist parents. Activities which stimulated mental or physical excitement were considered sinful by their elders, and Tituba's vivid stories of sorcery and the black arts doubtless provided an enthralling if impious outlet for the repressed adolescent feelings and imaginations of the young people.

The First Meeting House in Salem Village
(courtesy of the Danvers Archival Center)

Site of the Parris Parsonage
(courtesy of the Danvers Archival Center)

Before long, however, youthful fantasies developed into highly emotional episodes with all the characteristics of hysteria—convulsive seizures, blasphemous screaming, or trancelike states. The bizarre behavior of Betty and Abigail soon attracted the attention of Mr. Parris. Deeply concerned, he summoned a Salem Village physician, Dr. Griggs. Seventeenth-century medicine was medieval in approach, and the doctor, unable to determine any *physical* cause for their illness, suggested that the girls had, by some mischance, fallen under Satan's influence. Unexplainable behavior, diseases, and misfortunes were, at that time, commonly believed to be the result of spiritual forces at work in the world.

It was thought that Satan could exercise his power through intermediaries or witches who had signed a covenant with him to perform his evil deeds. These witches frequently assumed the guise of an individual known to the afflicted person appearing in a dream or vision to harm or

Recently Discovered Artifacts from the Parris Site
(courtesy of the Danvers Archival Center)

threaten that person. Often the witch was accompanied by a diabolical spirit called a "familiar," a small domestic animal—a dog, cat, bird, or even a grotesque creature with strange physical attributes such as the head of a woman and feathered wings. These phenomena were generally observed only by the bewitched victim and not by others in the vicinity. According to the legal and religious authorities, the Devil could not adopt the shape of an innocent person; therefore the people who appeared in the frightening visions were suspected of having contracted with Satan, and accounts of their appearances were considered "spectral evidence" of their guilt.

Following Dr. Griggs's evaluation of Abigail and Betty, the Reverend Mr. Parris called upon his church colleagues to assist in defeating the wicked spirits which had possessed the girls. Ministers from Salem Town, Beverly, and other communities convened in the Village to lead a public day of fasting and prayer, and to question the afflicted girls about what had caused their disturbing behavior. Clergymen Nicholas Noyes (Salem), John Hale (Beverly), and Deodat Lawson (formerly of the Village) were among the ministers conducting the investigation. The mysterious symptoms had affected several girls, including the

two from the Parris household and three from the family of Thomas Putnam, Jr., and a few older women as well.

Those stricken, in addition to Betty and Abigail, were:

Sarah Bibber, 36
Elizabeth Booth, 18
Sarah Churchill, 20, servant of George Jacobs, Sr.
Elizabeth Hubbard, 17, niece of Dr. Griggs
Mercy Lewis, 19, servant of Thomas Putnam
Gertrude Pope, of middle age
Ann Putnam, Sr., wife of Thomas Putnam
Ann Putnam, Jr., 12
Susannah Sheldon, 18
Mary Walcott, 17, daughter of Capt. Jonathan Walcott
Mary Warren, 20, servant of John Procter

These girls and women exhibited strange behavior—choking; apparent loss of speech, sight, and hearing; muscle spasms and fits; inability to pray; and at times, "spells" during which they saw vivid and frightening apparitions. They claimed these visions pursued them, threatening, biting, pinching, pricking, and performing other bodily injuries.* Coaxed to reveal the names of those who were tormenting them, the girls at first would not respond, but eventually they named three local women. Tituba the slave was one of those. Sarah Good, a housewife from a poor laboring family who had the reputation of a nagging shrew was the second. The third person charged was Sarah Osborne (or Osburn, Osburne), the prosperous widow of Robert Prince. Her unseem-

*On 25 February Mary Sibley, aunt of Mary Walcott, resorted to an old English tradition and had Tituba bake a "witch cake" made of rye meal mixed with the urine of the afflicted girls. The cake was then fed to the Parris dog on the assumption that if the girls were truly bewitched, the dog would manifest the same symptoms of torment. Mr. Parris was horrified by this experiment and denounced Mrs. Sibley from his pulpit for "going to the Devil for help against the Devil."

ly behavior prior to her second marriage to Alexander Osborne and her repeated absences from church services in recent months had been the subject of much gossip in the community.

On 29 February warrants were issued for the arrest of the three women, and during the next few days they were examined by two local magistrates, Jonathan Corwin and John Hathorne (an ancestor of author Nathaniel Hawthorne). Sarah Good and Sarah Osborne denied their guilt, but the emotional girls repeated their hysterical accusations during the examinations. Only Tituba confessed, admitting to having seen the Devil with four witches, two of whom she recognized as Good and Osborne. The three accused women were sent to a Boston jail to await formal trial. Their removal did not mean that Salem's witchcraft troubles were over, however. The girls continued their strange behavior, attributing their persistent ailments to other "agents" of the Devil. In the next few weeks more were accused and jailed: Martha Cory, Rebecca Nurse, Bridget Bishop, and little Dorcas Good.

Dorcas, the five-year-old daughter of Sarah Good, was accused by the girls of appearing in spectral form and biting them as revenge for her mother's incarceration. Dorcas was also deemed a witch and was confined in prison for four or five months. Eventually she was released, but the experience so affected her that she could never again function on a normal level, having, as her father reported, "little or no reason."

For many years, the Putnam family had been involved in boundary disputes with the family of Rebecca Nurse; perhaps it is not surprising that the visions of Ann Putnam, Sr., revealed to her that Rebecca's malevolence had caused the death of fourteen Putnam friends and relatives.

During the hearings of the accused witches, other citizens came forward and testified that they, too, had been personally harmed, had suffered damages to crops and livestock, or had re-

The Home of Jonathan Corwin,
Where Some of the Hearings Took Place

The Home of Rebecca Nurse in Danvers
(courtesy of the Danvers Archival Center)

HENRY RUTKOWSKI

9

ceived menacing midnight visits from the defendants—or from other persons in the community who might also be "servants of the devil." By early April, in an increasing atmosphere of suspicion and fear, the witchcraft epidemic had spread to nearby communities. Examinations took place in Salem Town before a larger group of magistrates, ministers, and even the deputy governor, and the number of suspects expanded. The afflicted girls had now achieved a certain notoriety, and they were asked to identify witches in other communities in Essex County. More than fifty persons were accused in the town of Andover alone.

One of those accused was the elderly John Alden of Boston, a prominent and wealthy fur merchant and the son of John and Priscilla. The Salem girls claimed he was the leader of the Boston witches. He was jailed, but after fifteen weeks in prison was able to escape to New York. He was cleared of the charge of witchcraft by the Superior Court in April 1693.

After preliminary hearings, most of those who were arrested were imprisoned and many were searched for "witchmarks"—warts or other physical blemishes from which, it was believed, the witches' "familiars" could suck nourishment.

On 10 May Sarah Osborne, ill, died in prison before she could be brought to trial. The jails were rapidly filling with those accused of witchcraft, but no trials could be held, owing to a legislative obstruction. Because of religious and politi-

Chief Justice William Stoughton
(courtesy of the Danvers Archival Center)

Justice Nathaniel Saltonstall
(courtesy of the Danvers Archival Center)

cal upheavals in England, Massachusetts had lost its charter as an independent commonwealth under the British Crown in 1684. No legislation could be negotiated until a new charter had been granted. The new charter was negotiated by the Reverend Increase Mather, father of Cotton Mather. It was finally granted by King William and Queen Mary, reaching Massachusetts in May 1692. The elder Mather was also influential in the Crown's appointment of the new governor of Massachusetts, Sir William Phips. Phips was a native-born American and a self-made man whose business successes in England had earned him a knighthood, granted by King James II in 1687.

At the end of May, Governor Phips, with the aid of his Council, set up a special court of Oyer and Terminer ("to hear and determine") in Salem and appointed as justices seven distinguished men with knowledge of the law. Lt. Gov. William Stoughton of Dorchester was named chief justice; other members of the court were Nathaniel Saltonstall (Haverhill), Bartholomew Gedney (Salem), and Samuel Sewall, John Richards, Wait Winthrop, and Peter Sergeant (Boston).

During interrogation, the magistrates based their evaluations on various kinds of "evidence." Most significant was direct *confession* by the accused person. *Supernatural attributes* were also considered important proofs—particularly the "witchmark" (any physical abnormality of the suspect) which was considered a sign of the devil's influence. Next most important were *superhuman feats* performed by the suspect—mind-reading or some physical phenomenon such as lifting an impossibly heavy object. *Empirical evidence* such as injury, illness, or property damage was regarded as reliable proof that the mischief was caused by a person with satanic powers. *Public tests*—observing the hysterical reactions of the afflicted girls as the judges questioned the "witches"—also offered significant evidence of guilt. Last, most controversial, and most relied upon by the court, was *spectral evidence,* which was either an "apparition" of the accused person attempting to cause some injury to the victim or the "specter" of a dead person who appeared in a vision and attributed his or her death to the accused.

11

The Court of Oyer and Terminer convened on 2 June, and on that day Bridget Bishop was sentenced to death by hanging.* The court also convened on 29 June with five convictions, on 5 August (six convictions), and twice in September (fifteen convictions). Of the twenty-seven convicted of witchcraft, nineteen were hanged. Giles Corey, one of the accused, actually pleaded "not guilty," but he subsequently refused to submit to a trial by jury. Legally, he could not then be convicted, but he was subjected to "peine forte et dure," an old outdated English common law which permitted placing stone weights upon the body of the accused until he died. Corey survived this horrible torture for two days before expiring.

The recorded examinations of Corey and others are poignant accounts of the courtroom ordeals suffered by the accused. Most of this testimony is fully covered in *The Salem Witchcraft Papers* (see bibliography) but for the purposes of this short booklet quoted excerpts from one case—that of Ann Pudeator—will illustrate the kind of harassment that the victims had to endure.**

*Following the death of Bridget Bishop on 10 June, Judge Saltonstall, "very much dissatisfyed with the proceedings," resigned from the court. He was replaced by Jonathan Corwin.

**For greater clarity, longer testimony excerpts have been set in italics and the spelling and punctuation of the excerpts have been adapted in this booklet to conform to more modern standards of English.

THE STORY OF ANN PUDEATOR

Ann Pudeator, a Salem widow, was arrested on 12 May 1692 and "charged with sundry acts of witchcraft committed this day contrary to the laws of our Sov'r Lord & Lady." The first witness to testify against Pudeator was Sarah Churchill, the twenty-year-old servant of George Jacobs, Sr. Sarah testified on 10 June that Pudeator "brought the book" to her, which Churchill said she signed. Then Churchill claimed the older woman conjured:

images like Mercy Lewis, Ann Putnam, Elizabeth Hubbard, and they brought her thorns and she stuck them in the images and told her [Sarah] the persons whose likenesses they were would be afflicted.

Warrant for the Arrest of Ann Pudeator, Signed by Corwin and Hathorne

13

Sketch of the Beadle Tavern
(courtesy of the Danvers Archival Center)

THOMAS BEADLE'S TAVERN, SALEM
Where many of those charged with witchcraft were examined
before trial

Ann Pudeator was examined by the magistrates on 2 July at the home of Thomas Beadle, at which time Sarah Churchill accused her directly: "You did bring me the book," and Pudeator responded that:

I never saw the woman before now. . . . I never saw the Devil's book nor knew that he had one.

One of the constables at the examination, Jeremiah Neal, was then asked what he knew of Ann Pudeator. He reported that Pudeator was:

an ill-carriaged woman; and since my wife has been sick of the smallpox, this woman has come to my house pretending kindness, and I was glad to see it. She asked whether she might use our mortar, which was used for my wife, and I consented to it, but I afterward repented of it, for the nurse told me my

wife was the worse . . . since she was very ill of a flux which she had not before. When the officer came for Pudeator, the nurse said, "You are come too late," for my wife grew worse till she died. . . . Pudeator had often threatened my wife.

Elizabeth Hubbard, seventeen, next testified that she had seen Ann Pudeator with Mary Walcott (one of the afflicted girls) and with Goody (Rebecca) Nurse, another suspected witch. Pudeator was then asked what she had done with the many ointments she had in her house and she replied:

I never had ointment nor oil but neatsfoot oil in my house since my husband died.

When Constable Neal disputed her statement, saying that nearly twenty containers of ointment or

14

grease had been found, she explained that she did have grease, but only to make soap of.

Sarah Bibber, thirty-six, was another of those at the hearing on 2 July. She said that she had never seen Pudeator prior to that day. Young Ann Putnam was then called upon. She said she had never seen Pudeator "prior to her last visit to Salem Town." At that point in the hearing, the scribe recorded that Ann Putnam:

fell into a fit, and Pudeator was commanded to take her by the wrist and did, and Putnam was well presently. Mary Warren fell into two fits quickly after one another, and both times was helped by Pudeator's taking her by the wrist.

On 5 September nine witnesses were summoned to the next Court of Oyer and Terminer in Salem to:

testify the truth to the best of their knowledge on certain indictments to be exhibited against Alice Parker [another witchcraft suspect] and Ann Pudeator.

At the trial, a formal indictment, signed by Mary Warren, Sarah Churchill, and Ann Putnam, was read:

The Jurors for our Sovereign Lord and Lady the King and Queen present that Ann Pudeator of Salem in the County of Essex, aforesaid widow, the second day of July in the year aforesaid and diverse other days and times as well before as after, certain detestable arts called witchcraft and sorceries wickedly, maliciously, and felloniously hath used, practiced, and exercised at and within the township of Salem aforesaid in and upon and against one Mary Warren of Salem, aforesaid single woman, by which said wicked acts the said Mary Warren the second day of July aforesaid and diverse other days and times both before and after was and is tortured, afflicted, pined, consumed, wasted, and tormented, and also for sun-

Pudeator Testimony: "I never saw the Devil's Book"

dry other acts of witchcraft by the said Ann Pudeator committed and done before and since that time against the peace of our Sovereign Lord and Lady the King and Queen, their crown and dignity, and against the form of the statute in that case made and provided.

On 6 September Sarah Churchill swore in the court record:

15

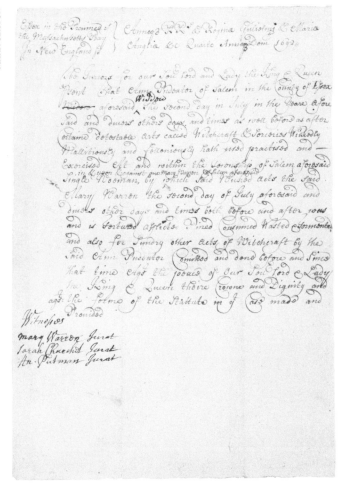

Mary Warren's accusation against Pudeator

Ann Pudeator hath often afflicted me by biting me, pinching me, sticking pins in me, and choking me; and particularly on the 2 day of July, at her examination, said Pudeator did afflict me greatly. Also she or her apparition did offer me the book to sign. . . . She told me also that she was the cause of John Turner's falling off the cherry tree to his great hurt and which amazed him in his head and almost killed him. She told me also she was the cause of Jeremiah Neal's wife's death, and I saw her hurt Elizabeth Hubbard, Mary Walcott, and Ann Putnam the last night. She afflicted me also last night by her witchcrafts and I do verily believe said Ann Pudeator is a witch.

Mary Warren also claimed that Pudeator had admitted killing her own husband and his first wife, and that she had been an "instrument" in the death of John Best's wife.

Mary Warren's testimony was followed by that of Elizabeth Hubbard, who swore that she had seen Ann Pudeator:

afflict Mary Warren and that she or her apparition did hurt me and Mary Warren the last night before the jury of inquest, and that she hath afflicted her since she came into court.

Twelve-year-old Ann Putnam was the next witness. She repeated the accusations of Warren and Hubbard, saying that she had seen Pudeator:

afflict Mary Warren, Mary Walcott, and Elizabeth Hubbard often, and particularly at the time of her last examination before the magistrates at Mr. Thomas Beadle's. She also hath afflicted me both then and at other times.

Several other witnesses testified against Ann Pudeator on 7 September. Sarah Bibber told the jury of inquest that she, too, had seen Pudeator afflict Warren, Walcott, and Putnam, that she her-

to the jury of inquest that Ann Pudeator has greatly afflicted her . . . by choking her, pinching her, and sticking pins into her, and by pressing of her and making her set her hand to the book . . . and brought poppets [dolls] to her to stick pins to, which she did. . . .

The next day Mary Warren, twenty, said upon oath to the jury that:

self had been afflicted, and that she believed Pudeator was a witch. Samuel Pickworth testified that about six weeks previously, he had been:

coming along Salem Street between Ann Pudeator's house and Captain Higginson's house, it being in the evening, and I . . . saw a woman near Captain Higginson's corner, the which I supposed to be Ann Pudeator, and in a moment of time she passed by me as swift as if a bird flew by me, and I saw the woman go in to Ann Pudeator's house.

Following this report, young Ann Putnam hastened to affirm to the jury that:

Ann Pudeator told her that she flew by a man in the night into a house.

The next witness was John Best, Sr., a forty-eight-year-old man who testified that some years before he had often heard his wife say:

that Ann Pudeator would not let her alone until she had killed her by her often pinching and bruising of her till her arms and other parts of her body looked black by reason of her sore pinching of her. In the time of her sickness, my wife did affirm that it was Ann Pudeator that afflict her, and stood in the belief of it as long as she lived.

Best's report was confirmed by his son, John Best, Jr., who claimed that his mother:

did several times in her sickness complain of Ann Pudeator of Salem, the wife of Jacob Pudeator, how she had bewitched her and that she did believe she would kill her before she had done; and so she said several times during her sickness, until her death. Also . . . I did several times go into the woods to fetch my father's cows, and I did drive Goody Pudeator's cow back from our cows, and I being all alone, Ann Pudeator would chide me when I came

Pudeator's Petition to the Judges

home for turning the cow back, by reason of which I . . . did conclude said Pudeator was a witch.

Three days later, on 10 September, Mary Walcott was the tenth and final witness to be called. She also claimed that Pudeator "afflicted" her and the Warren and Putnam girls, and said that she believed Pudeator was a witch. Following the trial, Ann Pudeator presented the following written petition to the court:

The humble petition of Ann Pudeator unto the honoured judge and bench now sitting in judicature in Salem humbly showeth: that whereas your poor and humble petitioner being condemned to die and knowing in my own conscience as I shall shortly answer it before the great God of heaven who is the searcher and knower of all hearts, that the evidence of John Best, Sr., and John Best, Jr., and Samuel Pickworth which was given in against me in court were all of them altogether false and untrue, and besides, the abovesaid John Best hath been formerly whipped and likewise is recorded for a liar, I would humbly beg of your honours to take it into your judicious and pious consideration that my life may not be taken away by such false evidence and witnesses as these be. Likewise, the evidence given in against me by Sarah Churchill and Mary Warren I am altogether ignorant of and know nothing in the least measure about it nor nothing else concerning the crime of witchcraft for which I am condemned to die, as will be known to men and angels at the great day of judgment begging and imploring your prayers at the throne of grace in my behalf, and your poor and humble petitioner shall for ever pray as she is bound in duty for your honours' health and happiness in this life and eternal felicity in the world to come.

It appears after reading the legal records of Ann Pudeator's trial that the evidence of her ten accusers was somewhat insubstantial. Several young women claimed that they had been bitten and pinched by her, that she had created "images" of people who would subsequently become ill, and that she had caused the witnesses to have fits in the courtroom. Others testified that Pudeator had caused the death of two sick women and injury to several other persons merely by being in their presence, that she possessed jars of magic oils and ointments, and that she (or someone who looked like her) had been seen "flying" in the twilight. The final declaration against her came from a young man who claimed Pudeator had scolded him for driving her cow back into the woods "by reason of which I did conclude that she was a witch."

From today's perspective, we would probably conclude that the most truthful and convincing document from Ann Pudeator's trial was her own humble petition on behalf of her innocence. A study of the trial manuscripts shows that the charges brought against Pudeator were similar in nature to much of the testimony recorded at the trials of other accused witches.

THE END OF THE TRIALS

By October of 1692 the Salem girls had accused, on spectral evidence, a number of prominent people, including (in addition to John Alden), Judge Nathaniel Saltonstall, the Reverend John Hale's wife, and Lady Phips, wife of the governor.

Rev. Increase Mather, president of Harvard College and the colony's ambassador to England, was a man prominent in ecclesiastical and public affairs, and he was deeply troubled by events in Salem. He wrote *Cases of Conscience Concerning Witchcrafts and Spirits Personating Men,* probably circulated in manuscript form in 1692. This document, published in 1693, disputed the validity of mere spectral evidence in determining guilt. "It were better that ten suspected witches should escape, than that one innocent person should be condemned," Increase Mather declared. "I had rather judge a witch to be an honest woman, than judge an honest woman as a witch." He went on to evaluate all of the accepted types of evidence, concluding that only two were valid proof of witchcraft: direct confession by the accused or the victim's testimony supported by two reliable witnesses. Increase Mather's son Cotton also continued to search for the causes and cure of the witchcraft affliction, but his attitude was more stringent than that of his father. The younger Mather urged vigorous prosecution of proven witches, but cautioned careful study of evidence. In 1693 he wrote an account of the trials, *Wonders of the Invisible World,* which was published and widely circulated. The book was an accurate and detailed history of the events of some of the trials, but unlike *Cases of Conscience,* it was flawed by his continuing belief that spectral evidence was in some cases authentic testimony and by his strong defense of the judges, who were by that time beginning to be criticized for the way they managed the trials.

A number of other writings on the witchcraft trials were circulated at that time. One was *A Modest Enquiry into the Nature of*

The Reverend Increase Mather
(courtesy of the Danvers Archival Center)

The Reverend Cotton Mather

A Modeſt Enquiry

Into the Nature of

Witchcraft,

AND

How Perſons Guilty of that Crime
may be *Convicted* : And the means
uſed for their Diſcovery Diſcuſſed,
both *Negatively* and *Affirmatively*,
according to *SCRIPTURE* and
EXPERIENCE.

By **John Hale**,

Paſtor of the Church of Chriſt in *Beverley*,
Anno Domini. 1 6 9 7.

*When they ſay unto you, ſeek unto them that have
Familiar Spirits and unto Wizzards that peep, &c.
To the Law and to the Teſtimony ; if they ſpeak
not according to this word, it is becauſe there is no
light in them,* Iſaiah VIII. 19, 20.
That which I ſee not teach thou me, Job 34 32.

BOSTON in N. E.
Printed by *B. Green,* and *J. Allen,* for
Benjamin Eliot under the Town Houſe: 1702

Title Page of John Hale's *A Modest Enquiry
Into the Nature of Witchcraft,*
printed in 1702

Witchcraft, written by Rev. John Hale in 1697
(although not published until 1702). Hale's was a
conservative account of the trials, concluding that
errors and mistakes had been made and that,
while witchcraft did exist, the 1692 affair had
been grossly distorted. Afflicted persons and the
magistrates, Hale said, had been deluded, and as a
result, many innocent victims had suffered.
Robert Calef, in *More Wonders of the Invisible
World* (1700), sharply attacked Cotton Mather's
volume and claimed that innocent blood had been

shed. Thomas Brattle, a scientist and Harvard
graduate, condemned the trial methods used by
the judges, declaring that they were unfair and
were based on superstition and ignorance. *A Brief
and True Narrative of some Remarkable Passages
Relating to sundry Persons Afflicted by Witchcraft
at Salem Village Which happened from the nine-
teenth of March to the Fifth of April, 1692* was a
brief report of the first-hand observations of
Deodat Lawson, the former Salem Village minister
who had been summoned by Samuel Parris to
assist in questioning the afflicted girls.

There were many hardships and injustices in-
flicted on those who were judged guilty of traf-
ficking with the Devil. First of all, those who
were jailed (or their families) were required to pay
the jailer for food and other services, even for the
chains which bound them. Over a period of weeks
and months the debts accrued as the prisoners
could not work at their accustomed trades or
chores to earn payment. Often their personal
property was confiscated to pay these fees. In addition, any person receiving a sentence of death
was subject to laws of "attainder"; that is, the
convicted individual lost his civil rights, and in a
sense, no longer had any legal rights. Some of
those who were convicted and jailed and later released suffered severe deprivation and were unable
to reclaim their property or legal rights for many
years, until the "attainders" were finally reversed
by court action.

Ironically, those who confessed to witchcraft
were generally not sent to the gallows. Their confessions, whether forced by physical means (several men were hanged by the heels until they admitted their guilt) or by verbal persuasion, were
followed by expressions of remorse and renuncia-
tion of the Devil. At this point the accusers frequently experienced a mysterious and immediate
relief from all symptoms. The presiding judges
granted a temporary reprieve to the confessors.
The small and courageous number who staunchly

defended their own innocence could not be co-erced into making false confessions and thereby lost their lives.

The final witchcraft hangings (seven women and one man) took place at Gallows Hill in Salem on 22 September 1692. In all, twenty-four people died as a result of the witchcraft trials. They were:

Bridget Bishop *(hanged)*
George Burroughs *(hanged)*
Martha Carrier *(hanged)*
Giles Corey, or Cory *(pressed to death)*
Martha Corey *(hanged)*
Lydia Dastin *(acquitted, but died in prison, unable to pay jail fees)*
Mary Easty, or Esty *(hanged)*
Ann Foster *(died in prison, following her confession)*
Sarah Good *(hanged)*
Sarah Good's unnamed infant *(died in prison)*
Elizabeth Howe *(hanged)*
George Jacobs, Sr. *(hanged)*
Susannah Martin *(hanged)*
Rebecca Nurse *(hanged)*
Sarah Osborne *(died in prison)*
Alice Parker *(hanged)*
Mary Parker *(hanged)*
John Procter, or Proctor *(hanged)*

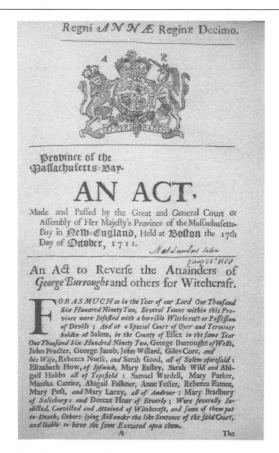

First Page of *An Act to Reverse the Attainders, 1711* (courtesy of the Danvers Archival Center)

Ann Pudeator *(hanged)*
Wilmot "Mammy" Redd *(hanged)*
Margaret Scott *(hanged)*
Samuel Wardwell *(hanged)*
Sarah Wildes *(hanged)*
John Willard *(hanged)*

None of those hanged had confessed to witchcraft, except Samuel Wardwell, who denied his guilt prior to his death.

Those who were convicted and sentenced but were granted temporary reprieves (and hence did not die) were:

Mary Bradbury *(escaped from prison)*
Rebecca Eames *(presumed to have confessed and was released)*
Abigail Faulkner *(released owing to pregnancy)*
Dorcas Hoar *(confessed)*
Abigail Hobbs *(presumed to have confessed and was released)*
Mary Lacy *(presumed to have confessed and was released)*
Elizabeth Procter *(released owing to pregnancy)*
Tituba *(confessed)*

Sarah Clayes (or Cloyse) was accused and imprisoned, but she escaped. Tituba was accused and jailed, but was ransomed in May of 1693 and probably remained a slave for the remainder of her life. One other woman was also released into servitude. Other persons who had been accused, imprisoned, and acquitted were obliged to remain in prison until their jail debts had been paid by friends and family.

On 26 October 1693 the Massachusetts legislature requested a convocation of ministers to advise the court on the disposition of those accused who were still in prison. Increase Mather led the group of ministers who urged that spectral accounts should no longer be considered valid testimony. He insisted on credible witnesses and re-jected the public tests of the afflicted people who demonstrated their persecution by bizarre behavior in front of the magistrates. He also questioned supposedly authentic empirical evidence—a squabble between two parties or a mischievous act by one of the parties against the other. The judges were advised to accept only direct confession and empirical proof of supernatural powers as true testimony, and it was stressed that the only reliable witnesses were persons of good reputation who would testify under oath.

When the newly appointed Superior Court of Judicature met in January of 1693, forty-nine of fifty-two accused persons were dismissed from prison on the grounds that evidence against them was insufficient to warrant trial. Elizabeth Johnson, Mary Post, and Sarah Wardwell were convicted, but some weeks later were freed by Governor Phips. He later pardoned all of the witchcraft accused who were still in jail and granted amnesty to those who had fled or escaped imprisonment.

*Additional information about Sarah Cloyce has been provided by Stephen W. Herring, curator of the Framingham (Massachusetts) Historical and Natural History Society. According to Josiah H. Temple's *History of Framingham* (Town of Framingham, 1887), Sarah, a sister of Rebecca Towne Nurse and Mary Easty, was tried and condemned to death and was confined in the Ipswich jail, but managed to escape. In the spring of 1693 she moved to Framingham with her family and other members of the Towne and Nurse families. They settled in a section of the reserved commons land later renamed "Salem End." Lt. Gov. Thomas Danforth had extensive land holdings in Framingham, and it is thought that he was probably involved in the resettlement of the Salem families.

THE AFTERMATH

For many years following the conclusion of the trials, the courts and churches declared days of penance and prayer in apology for the injustices done. In January 1696 twelve of the witch trial jurors signed a statement of contrition, admitting that

we confess that we our selves were not capable to understand, nor able to withstand the mysterious delusions of the Powers of Darkness, and Prince of the Air; but were for want of Knowledge in our selves and better information from others, prevailed with to take up such evidence against the Accused, as on further consideration, and better Information we justly fear was insufficient. . . .

Trial Judge *Samuel Sewall,* painted by John Smibert

The following year, on 14 January 1697, the first formal fast-day was held. On that day Judge Samuel Sewall, repenting his role in the trials, publicly declared in church his feelings of "blame and shame" and asked God to pardon him for his sins. Other personages involved in the trials later expressed remorse. Even Ann Putnam, Jr., one of the principal accusers, confessed in 1706 that she had been deluded by the Devil, and she publicly acknowledged her share of responsibility for "the guilt of innocent blood." Ann never married, but most of the other afflicted girls eventually were wed and gradually moved away from Salem Village to start new lives. Increasingly unpopular in his parish, Samuel Parris resigned his ministry in 1697 and moved to Boston and then to Sudbury, where he died in 1720. Parris was replaced in the meeting house by a young man named Joseph Green, a pastor who helped to restore peace and stability to the parish. In 1752 Salem Village finally was permitted to separate from Salem Town and adopted the name of Danvers.

In 1709 twenty-one of the survivors and families of those accused petitioned the court for redress of the loss of their civil rights and property. Cotton Mather supported their plea, and in 1711 the General Court reversed the attainders and legal restrictions which had been placed upon the victims and ordered that all petitions be compensated. Five hundred and ninety-eight pounds was repaid to the petitioners, in varying amounts—small recompense for all they had suffered. Even as recently as 1957, some of the heirs of Ann Pudeator raised the issue in the courts once again, and the General Court passed a Resolve (28 August 1957) that "Ann Pudeator and certain other persons" may have been illegally tried according to a "shocking" law of the time and that therefore the descendants of the accused witches should at long last be absolved of their burden of inherited guilt and shame.

The phenomenon of witchcraft has been studied by many historians, and a number of theories about its occurrence have evolved. Even during the early period of the Salem trials it was said by some contemporary observers that tales of witchcraft were based on nothing more than idle gossip. More recent scholars have noted that episodes of witchcraft, both in Europe and America, follow closely a period of social or political unrest. In the sixteenth and early seventeenth centuries, Europe was evolving from an agrarian to a more industrial capitalistic system. The shift from a peasant society of small villages and neighborly ways to a more aggressive individualistic economy created tensions and jealousies as some people gained personal successes and others slipped into deeper poverty. This state of uneasiness created a climate of suspicion and helped to generate accusations of witchcraft between rival factions.

In New England similar social and economic changes took place in the mid- to late 1600s. Salem Town in particular had grown as a shipping and mercantile center, whereas Salem Village was a smaller and for the most part less well-to-do agricultural hamlet. Conflict between the two communities was perhaps inevitable. In addition to these strains, there were controversies between religious and political groups and the inevitable friction between several generations of people living in close contact with one another. The emotional extremes of the girls which erupted into hysterical behavior have been attributed by some to adolescent overreaction. Others claim that the presence of a fungus (ergot) in local bread may have caused the delusions of the afflicted ones. Perhaps the Salem witchcraft explosion was a culmination of all of these factors.

In retrospect it can be said that the infamous witch trials of 1692 are an unforgettable part of Salem's long history. Although it is not a chapter to be proud of, that portion of the record nevertheless does more than merely chronicle the events in one troubled community. The Salem witchcraft story reflects the problems, beliefs, and attitudes of an era and demonstrates the desperate struggle of a society to resolve a terrifying crisis by the best legal and moral means available at the time.

MEMORABILIA OF THE
WITCHCRAFT TRIALS OF 1692

Memorabilia associated with the trials are collected and treasured in Salem, and although original artifacts are scarce, a number of authentic items have been acquired by the Peabody Essex Museum, the Danvers Archival Center, and other local organizations. The Peabody Essex owns a trunk belonging originally to Jonathan Corwin, a Salem Town magistrate, who shared with John Hathorne the initial responsibility for hearing the testimony at the preliminary witchcraft hearings on 1 March 1692. Corwin's house, where some of the deliberations took place, still stands at the corner of Essex and North Streets, and is shown in an 1819 painting by Samuel Bartoll that hangs in the Peabody Essex Museum. A portrait by John Smibert of Samuel Sewall, one of the trial magistrates, may be found in the Museum's portrait collection.

The Witch House, painted by Samuel Bartoll, 1819.

Mary Hollingsworth (or Holingworth) English stitched a handsome sampler (c. 1665–1670, now in the Museum collections) some twenty years before she was accused of witchcraft along with her wealthy husband, Philip. They were among the fortunate ones who avoided imprisonment, fleeing to New York, where they were guests of the governor until the trials ended. Philip English later petitioned the court for 1500 pounds for property confiscated at the time of his imprisonment, but the court awarded him nothing. Mary's sampler, Philip's chair and cane, and a piece of a seventeenth-century bottle impressed "Phillip English" are also at the Peabody Essex Museum, as is the brass sundial belonging to John Procter, the farmer accused and later hanged as a witch. Procter is a central figure in Arthur Miller's stunning play about the trials, *The Crucible*.

Two of George Jacobs's canes are owned by the Peabody Essex, and one of the canes was used as a model in the nineteenth-century painting of *The Trial of George Jacobs*, a feature of the Museum's

Sampler Worked
by Mary Hollingsworth
(English)

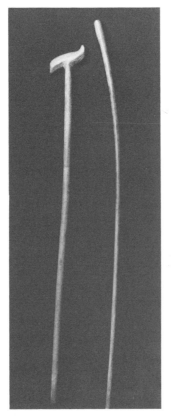

Two of George Jacobs's Canes

Sketch of the Philip English House

popular exhibition of the witchcraft trials. Jacobs was hanged on 19 August 1692. Although he denied that he was a witch, he was convicted on evidence that he could not recite the Lord's Prayer and because a blemish on his shoulder was considered a "true mark" of the Devil. Other artifacts at the Museum include a tiny bottle containing finger bones supposed to be those of Jacobs, a section of an old coffin (perhaps of another unlucky victim) unearthed some years ago at Salem's Gallows Hill, nails from the Corwin house, a wooden peg from the house of George Jacobs, and

George Jacobs's House

Sundial Owned
by John Procter

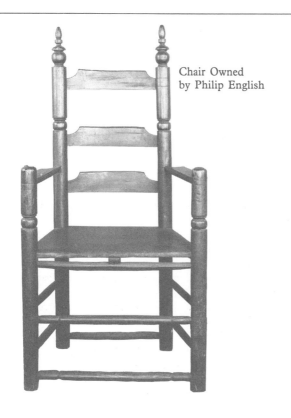

Chair Owned
by Philip English

valuable relics of the witchcraft trials are the accounts of the trials themselves, handwritten by court scribes as the proceedings took place. These remarkable documents, some 552 in all, are securely stored in the library of the Peabody Essex under temperature-controlled conditions. Twenty-five of the manuscripts are owned by the Museum, and 527 were restored by the Social Law Library Colonial Court Records Project (Boston) and placed at the Museum on permanent deposit in 1980 by the Essex County, Massachusetts, Court. Known collectively as "The Salem Witchcraft Papers," the manuscripts provide a fascinating chronology of the trials, including records of declarations, arrest warrants, indictments, examinations of the afflicted and the accused, complaints, accounts, petitions for acquittal or conviction, summonses, mittimuses (writs instructing jailers to hold prisoners), and death warrants. Documents displayed in the witchcraft exhibition have included such items as the warrant for the arrest of Martha Corey "for suspition of haveing Comitted sundry acts of Witchcraft" and the deposition of Mercy Lewis against Giles Corey claiming that the "Apperishtion" of the old man had tried to force her to sign his book by beating and torturing her. These priceless accounts are poignant testimony to a dramatic and unforgettable episode in American history.

timbers from the old Salem jail (located at the corner of St. Peter Street and Federal Street), which housed the unfortunates as they awaited trial. A somewhat gruesome memento is a collection of "witch pins," preserved with the court records and purportedly used by the accused to torment the witch victims.

Special attractions at the Peabody Essex Museum are the two large paintings, *The Trial of George Jacobs, August 5, 1692* (previously mentioned) and *Examination of a Witch*, painted by Tompkins Harrison Matteson in the 1850s. These canvases are dramatic recreations of the trials by a noted nineteenth-century painter of the American "romantic" school. The paintings are reproduced on the front and back covers of this booklet.

As has been noted, the most important and

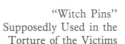

"Witch Pins"
Supposedly Used in the
Torture of the Victims

SELECT BIBLIOGRAPHY

Aylesworth, Thomas G. *Servants of the Devil.* Reading, Mass.: Addison-Wesley Publishing Company, Inc., 1970.

Burr, George Lincoln, ed. *Narratives of the Witchcraft Cases, 1648–1706.* New York: Charles Scribner's Sons, 1914.

Boyer, Paul, and Stephen Nissenbaum. *Salem Possessed: The Social Origins of Witchcraft.* Cambridge, Massachusetts, and London, England: Harvard University Press, 1974.

Boyer, Paul, and Stephen Nissenbaum. *The Salem Witchcraft Papers,* 3 vols. New York: DaCapo Press, 1977.

Demos, John Putnam. *Entertaining Satan. Witchcraft and the Culture of Early New England.* New York: Oxford University Press, Inc., 1982.

Hansen, Chadwick. *Witchcraft at Salem.* New York: G. Braziller, 1969. Reprint. New York: a Mentor Book from the New American Library, 1969.

Levin, David. *What Happened in Salem?* New York: Harcourt, Brace & World, Inc., 1960.

Miller, Arthur. *The Crucible, A Play in Four Acts.* New York: Viking Press, 1953.

Nevins, Winfield S. *Witchcraft in Salem Village in 1692.* Salem: The Salem Press Co., 1916.

Powers, Edwin. *Crime and Punishment in Early Massachusetts, 1620–1692.* Boston: Beacon Press, 1966.

Robbins, Rossell Hope. *The Encyclopedia of Witchcraft and Demonology.* New York: Crown Publishers, Inc., 1970.

Starkey, Marion L. *The Devil in Massachusetts.* New York: A. A. Knopf, 1949. Reprint. Garden City, N.Y.: Anchor Books, Doubleday & Company, Inc., 1969.

Trask, Richard B. *Salem Village and the Witch Hysteria.* New York: Grossman Publishers, Viking Press, 1975.

Upham, Charles N. *Salem Witchcraft,* 2 vols. Boston: Wiggin and Lunt, 1867. Reprint. New York: Frederick Ungar Publishing Company, 1976.